MOVIE FAVORITES

Solos and Band Arrangements
Correlated with Essential Elements Band Method

Arranged by
MICHAEL SWEENEY

T0052820

Welcome to Essential Elements Movie Favorites! There are two versions of each selection in this versatile book. The SOLO version appears on the left-hand page of your book. The FULL BAND arrangement appears on the right-hand page. Optional accompaniment recordings are available separately in CD or cassette format. Use these recordings when playing solos for friends and family.

ISBN 978-0-7935-5964-0

HAL•LEONARD™
CORPORATION
7777 W. BLUEMOUND RD. P.O. BOX 13819 MILWAUKEE, WI 53213

00860020

From The Universal Motion Picture JURASSIC PARK

Theme From "JURASSIC PARK"

BARITONE T.C.
Solo

Composed by JOHN WILLIAMS
Arranged by MICHAEL SWEENEY

MCA music publishing

From The Universal Motion Picture JURASSIC PARK

Theme From "JURASSIC PARK"

BARITONE T.C.
Band Arrangement

Composed by JOHN WILLIAMS
Arranged by MICHAEL SWEENEY

MCA music publishing

00860020

From CHARIOTS OF FIRE

CHARIOTS OF FIRE

BARITONE T.C.
Solo

Music by VANGELIS
Arranged by MICHAEL SWEENEY

00860020

CHARIOTS OF FIRE

BARITONE T.C.
Band Arrangement

Music by VANGELIS
Arranged by MICHAEL SWEENEY

From THE MAN FROM SNOWY RIVER

THE MAN FROM SNOWY RIVER

(Main Title Theme)

BARITONE T.C
Solo

By BRUCE ROWLAND
Arranged by MICHAEL SWEENEY

00860020

From The Paramount Motion Picture FORREST GUMP

FORREST GUMP - MAIN TITLE

(Feather Theme)

BARITONE T.C.
Solo

Music by ALAN SILVESTRI
Arranged by MICHAEL SWEENEY

From The Paramount Motion Picture FORREST GUMP

FORREST GUMP - MAIN TITLE
(Feather Theme)

BARITONE T.C.
Band Arrangement

Music by ALAN SILVESTRI
Arranged by MICHAEL SWEENEY

00860020

From AN AMERICAN TAIL

SOMEWHERE OUT THERE

**Words and Music by JAMES HORNER,
BARRY MANN and CYNTHIA WEIL**

Arranged by MICHAEL SWEENEY

BARITONE T.C.
Solo

MCA music publishing

SOMEWHERE OUT THERE

BARITONE T.C.
Band Arrangement

Words and Music by JAMES HORNER,
BARRY MANN and CYNTHIA WEIL
Arranged by MICHAEL SWEENEY

Moderately Slow

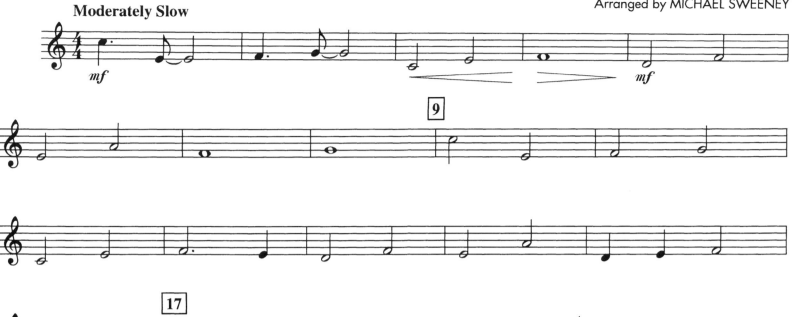

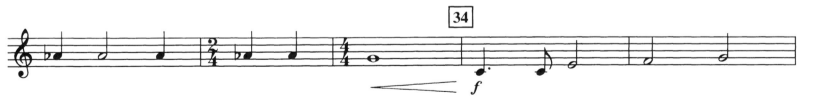

MCA music publishing

From DANCES WITH WOLVES

THE JOHN DUNBAR THEME

BARITONE T.C.
Solo

By JOHN BARRY
Arranged by MICHAEL SWEENEY

From **DANCES WITH WOLVES**

THE JOHN DUNBAR THEME

BARITONE T.C.
Band Arrangement

By JOHN BARRY
Arranged by MICHAEL SWEENEY

Expressively

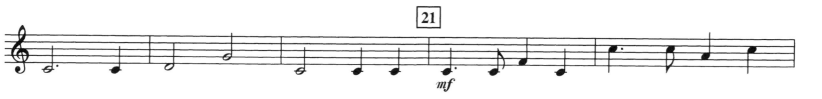

From The Paramount Motion Picture RAIDERS OF THE LOST ARK

RAIDERS MARCH

BARITONE T.C.
Solo

By JOHN WILLIAMS
Arranged by MICHAEL SWEENEY

RAIDERS MARCH

BARITONE T.C.
Band Arrangement

By JOHN WILLIAMS
Arranged by MICHAEL SWEENEY

00860020

From APOLLO 13
APOLLO 13
(End Credits)

By JAMES HORNER
Arranged by MICHAEL SWEENEY

BARITONE T.C.
Solo

MCA music publishing

From APOLLO 13
APOLLO 13
(End Credits)

By JAMES HORNER
Arranged by MICHAEL SWEENEY

BARITONE T.C.
Band Arrangement

MCA music publishing

00860020

From The Universal Picture E.T. (THE EXTRA-TERRESTRIAL)

THEME FROM E.T. (THE EXTRA-TERRESTRIAL)

BARITONE T.C.
Solo

Music by JOHN WILLIAMS
Arranged by MICHAEL SWEENEY

MCA music publishing

00860020

From The Universal Picture E.T. (THE EXTRA-TERRESTRIAL)

THEME FROM E.T. (THE EXTRA-TERRESTRIAL)

19

BARITONE T.C.
Band Arrangement

Music by JOHN WILLIAMS
Arranged by MICHAEL SWEENEY

Energetically

Broadly

Tempo I

MCA music publishing

Theme From The Paramount Picture STAR TREK

STAR TREK®-THE MOTION PICTURE

BARITONE T.C.
Solo

Music by JERRY GOLDSMITH
Arranged by MICHAEL SWEENEY

00860020

STAR TREK®-THE MOTION PICTURE

BARITONE T.C.
Band Arrangement

Music by JERRY GOLDSMITH
Arranged by MICHAEL SWEENEY

From The Universal Motion Picture BACK TO THE FUTURE

BACK TO THE FUTURE

BARITONE T.C.
Solo

By ALAN SILVESTRI
Arranged by MICHAEL SWEENEY

MCA music publishing

00860020

From The Universal Motion Picture BACK TO THE FUTURE

BACK TO THE FUTURE

BARITONE T.C.
Band Arrangement

By ALAN SILVESTRI
Arranged by MICHAEL SWEENEY

00860020

MCA music publishing

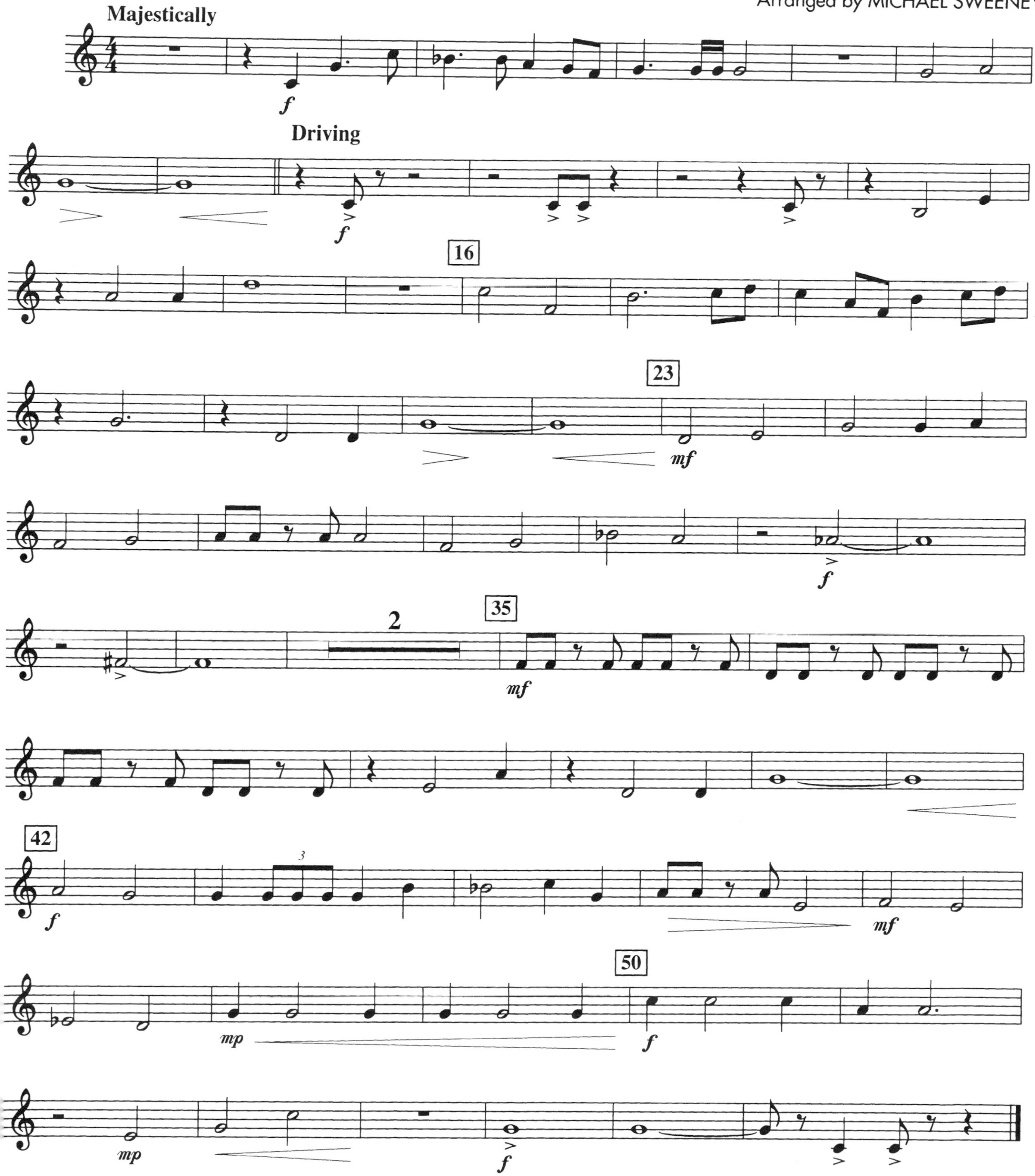